Marriage Bliss

Marriage Bliss

DICK MILLS

W *Whitaker House*

Unless otherwise indicated, all Scripture quotations are taken from the *King James Version* (KJV) of the Bible.

MARRIAGE BLISS

Dick Mills
Dick Mills Ministries, Inc.
P.O. Box 2600
Orange, CA 92669

ISBN: 0-88368-394-6
Printed in the United States of America
Copyright © 1983 by Dick Mills

Whitaker House
580 Pittsburgh Street
Springdale, PA 15144

2 3 4 5 6 7 8 9 10 11 12 13 / 06 05 04 03 02 01 00 99 98 97 96

Contents

Introduction

In the world today there is a shabby attitude toward the subject of marriage. There are very few real love songs or stories anymore. Everything written is sordid. This is an unfortunate thing.

When I grew up, the romantic syndrome was prevalent. The classic love story was this:

Prince Charming comes charging up on his horse to the castle where Sleeping Beauty lies. He jumps off his horse and swims across the moat. Sweeping into the castle, he searches for and finds Sleeping Beauty. When he kisses her, she awakens and recognizes him as her love. He picks her up and whisks her out of the castle. Holding her up, he swims across the moat, lifts her onto his horse, and together they ride off to live happily ever after.

Stories like this one are hardly written anymore.

In the modern version, the hero reaches the castle to find that some radical has blown it up.

Or . . . he reaches the castle, finds Sleeping Beauty, and kisses her—but she is "stoned" on drugs and doesn't wake up. The hero tries to wake her up but can't, so he just gives up and says, "Forget it. I'll just find some other girl."

Or . . . Sleeping Beauty wakes up when the hero kisses her, but says to him, "I'm not interested in you, sonny. I've got a girl friend."

Or . . . the story proceeds as in the classic version, but when the hero tries to swim the two of them across the moat, he drowns.

We need to change our attitude toward love and marriage. We need to go back to the way it was in the beginning, the way God meant it to be. Love and marriage should be like hearts and flowers. The heart pumps with joy in a marriage blessed of God. Flowers add color and aroma to an existence that would otherwise be drab and colorless. Marriage adds that dimension of color and aroma to a life that would otherwise be colorless. Hearts and flowers equal heartbeat, color, and fragrance.

1
Two Are Better Than One

Ecclesiastes 4:9-12 says:

Two are better than one; because they have a good reward for their labour. For if they fall, the one will lift up his fellow: but woe to him that is alone when he falleth; for he hath not another to help him up.

Again, if two lie together, then they have heat: but how can one be warm alone? And if one prevail against him, two shall withstand him; and a threefold cord is not quickly broken.

Jesus sent His disciples out two by two. (Mark 6:7.) Deuteronomy 32:30 says one person should *chase a thousand* (stand against a thousand discouraging things), but two can put *ten thousand* (discouraging things) *to flight*. Notice how the arithmetic changes. One can stand against *one* thousand; two can stand against *ten* thousand.

Husbands should say to their wives, "You're worth nine thousand to me." (This amount in dollars wouldn't be tax deductible, but a wife is worth much more than that!)

Wives should answer their husbands with kind words. Amos 3:3 says, *Can two walk together, except they be agreed?* Can two people go through life unless they are in harmony?

It's Not Good
For the Man to be Alone

On the first day of creation God looked at everything and said, "It's good." On the second and third days He said, "It's good." On the fourth, fifth, and sixth days, He said, "It's good." But then God noticed something about His creation that wasn't good.

In the Garden of Eden God had created and paired off birds, fish, and beasts of the field in male and female. But the man Adam had been created alone. The Lord looked down at Adam and said, *It is not good that man should be alone . . .* (Gen. 2:18). Loneliness is the first thing God pronounced as disastrous to humanity (and it is still a major problem today.) So God said, *. . . I will make him an help meet for him.*

With that, God performed the first wedding ceremony. After putting a deep sleep on Adam, He removed one of Adam's ribs and made a wife out of the rib. (Gen. 2:21,22.)

God made Adam from the dust of the earth, but He didn't make Eve this way. If He had, Eve would have been an independent entity. When God made Eve from Adam's rib, He created a mutual interdependency. Neither Adam nor Eve was complete without the other.

The Septuagint Bible[1], a Greek translation of the Old Testament by Charles Thomson, says that when God put a deep sleep on Adam, he was in a state of *ecstasis*. From *ecstasis* we get our word *ecstasy*. What happened to Adam while he slept was not a painful thing. The Helen Spurrell translation[2] of the Old Testament says he was in a trance. While Adam was asleep, God was literally tickling his ribs.

In Proverbs 5:18 we see the attitude a man should have toward his wife: . . . *rejoice with the wife of thy youth*. Ecclesiastes 9:9 says, *Live joyfully with the wife whom thou lovest all the days of the life of thy vanity . . . .*

Being a semanticist, I love to do research on words and find their implications. According to *The Exhaustive Concordance of The Bible*[3] by James Strong, one Hebrew word for joy is *gheel* which means "to spin around under the influence of any violent emotion." Although *gheel* is not the word used in Ecclesiastes 9:9, the idea is there for a husband to get happy, to get excited, to spin around like a top.

I've never seen a man spin like a top because he's married. In fact, I've heard some men call their wives "the warden" (and some women call their husbands "the old man"). Wedlock is not padlock! Comments like this should not be made because *two are better than one.*

Adam was in a state of ecstasy, happy about the creation of Eve. According to *The Living Bible*[4], Adam took one look at Eve and said, "This is it!" (Gen. 2:23). Never did he say to God, "I want my rib back!"

2

The Purpose of Marriage

Some churches claim that the only purpose for marriage is reproduction. They see the woman as some kind of baby machine.

Then the pendulum swings to the other extreme, where people believe the only purpose for marriage is sensual gratification. The population explosion has caused many radical abortionists and conservationists to want reproduction eliminated altogether.

What is the purpose of marriage?

We can answer this question by examining in greater detail the relationship between Adam and Eve.

"Multiply"

God said to Adam and Eve, *Be fruitful, and multiply, and replenish the earth* (Gen. 1:28). In these words, God declares marriage to be the legitimate way of producing, protecting, and raising children to face an adult world. This verse reveals something else: A married couple that does not reproduce can be missing the real purpose of marriage.

Many women have shed tears over their inability to have children. Women who never bear children are like ships that never go to sea. We should have compassion for couples who would like to have children but can't.

"An Help Meet"

It's a sad thing when a couple goes through life without having children. But did God mean for reproduction to be the *only* reason for a husband and wife to have sexual relations? To answer this, let's first examine the meaning of the word *help meet*.

The English word, *help meet*, is ambiguous. But the Hebrew word for help meet, *ezer-kenegdo*, actually means "a counterpart."

According to several lexicons, *help meet* means "one who stands in the front of and looks into the eyes of."

The center references of the older Bibles describe *help meet* as "one to meet him face to face; one to see him eye to eye." The woman is to stand and look straight into the eyes of the man.

Think about the ways other creatures reproduce: fish spawn, deer and other animals mate, birds lay and hatch eggs. In the whole creation of nature, man is the only creature for which a face-to-face confrontation during copulation is natural.

First Samuel 16:7 states: . . . *for man looketh on the outward appearance, but the Lord looketh on the heart.* The first part of the above verse in the original Hebrew says, "man looks into the eyes." Someone once said that the eyes are the windows to the soul. The eyes are very expressive.

Adam was not complete until he had a mate. When Adam and Eve looked into each other's eyes, they found fulfillment.

Another meaning of *help meet* is "alter ego." Alter ego is "the other self." Psychiatrists have been looking for the other self within us while the Bible states that the wife is the other self. When a man says about his wife, "This is my better half," he isn't far from expressing the truth in this principle.

When God said, "I'm going to give Adam an *ezer-kenegdo*," He was saying,

"I'm going to make for him an alter ego, the other self; one who will be his sexual counterpart, one who will face him and look into his eyes."

A Unique Relationship

Second, notice that humans are also unique in that they possess the ability to have relations at will.

Christian sociologists point out that animals can mate only at particular times. Fish have a spawning season that varies with the species; for instance, rainbow trout spawn in May, brown trout in November. Deer mate in late winter. In the middle of March the robins fly to a warmer climate where the female builds a nest and lays her eggs. To every inferior creature there is a season known as the mating season.

God created Adam and Eve to have face-to-face confrontation. He also made it possible for them to have relations at any time by an act of the will. God meant for there to be much more to marriage than reproduction.

There was a belief held by people of polytheistic religions that if they enjoyed life too much, some jealous deity might strike them dead. As a result, the non-Christian world was seized by a tyrannical fear making it impossible for a man and a woman to really enjoy each other or their children. This pagan idea has crept into Christianity. Many Christians think: *If I'm too happy in life, somebody up there is going to get jealous and zap me!*

People who have carried this belief into their marriages, homes, and families don't know how to enjoy anything. They are horribly afraid that if they do enjoy something, somebody will take it away from them.

This pagan concept does not line up with what God has told us life should be like. God meant for husbands and wives to find a great dimension of fulfillment in each other, as is expressed in this thought:

Woman was made from the rib of a man. She was not created from his head to top him, nor from his feet to be stepped on. She was made from his side to be equal to him; from beneath his arm to be protected by him; near his heart to be loved by him.

A friend who was working on his master's degree told me about a paper he wrote. In it he said:

"I met my wife at a beach in Santa Monica. She had a nice shape; I had bulging muscles. She thought I was handsome; I thought she was good-looking—so we got married. We had a one-third marriage. It was just a physical union.

"One day we went to church and heard the Gospel. We responded to the altar call and received Christ. That gave us a two-thirds marriage, a union of body and soul. Our souls were in union, because we had become Christians.

"In church ten years later, we both were filled with the Holy Spirit and spoke in tongues. Now we have a three-thirds marriage, a union of spirit, soul, and body. Until you're filled with the Holy Ghost and speak in tongues, you aren't married."

My friend firmly believes that God means for a husband and wife to find fulfillment in each other. The paper he wrote was for a marriage counseling class!

One night as the moon was shining in the Garden of Eden, Eve was feeling romantic, so she snuggled close to Adam. With her eyes twinkling, she asked, "Adam, do you love me?" Adam answered, "Who else?"

Adam didn't have much choice. But the point of this story is that God intended for Adam and Eve to find fulfillment in each other.

God means for a husband and wife to reproduce. But He also means for them to have a beautiful relationship of happiness, contentment, fulfillment, and meaning.

3

Love in Marriage

The Victorian Age perpetrated some ideas which have distorted our view of love in marriage.

The Victorians felt that a groomed and cultured woman should show no desire. They felt that she should be a sort of passive recipient. These attitudes produced frigidity and a general sense of shame concerning the act of love in marriage. Sex was a dirty word. Lovemaking was some filthy, naughty thing that caused guilt and condemnation. This attitude is not right.

Mutual Love

Both the Old and New Testaments reveal that God considers love in marriage to be normal and *mutual*. (The Greek word for this type of love is *eros*.) He made it to be wholesome, balanced, and equal.

In the Old Testament we read that God said to Eve, *. . . thy desire shall be to thy husband* (Gen. 3:16).

Daniel 11:37 refers to *the desire of women*. I looked up this phrase in several Hebrew lexicons, which were written by nineteenth and early twentieth century men who spoke Elizabethan English. The people living then chose more delicate words than we usually do today. But the lexicographers wrote plainly that God put in every woman's heart the desire to be loved by a man, to have a child in her womb, and to nurse a child at her breast. They stated that this desire is normal.

In the New Testament we read that Paul said, *The wife hath not power of her own body, but the husband: and likewise*

also the husband hath not power of his own
body, but the wife (1 Cor. 7:4).

God created in both male and female
an equally intense desire for love in
marriage. We can see that the Victorians
distorted the truth. Women are just
now emerging from these Victorian
attitudes.

The Union
of Christ and the Church

Jesus called God "Father."

The Holy Spirit is like the mother.
Everything the mother does, the Holy
Spirit does: consoles, comforts, guides,
stands by, encourages. He picks us up
when we fall. The ministry of the Holy
Spirit is the same as a mother's to a
child.

Jesus called Himself "the
Bridegroom."

In God there is the Father, Mother,
and Son. The Son is going to have a

bride. The Bible likens the Church to a Bride.

Three of Jesus' approximately thirty parables have to do with the marriage of the King's Son and His Bride. The book of Revelation gives an invitation to a wedding in the skies between Christ and His Bride.

Let us be glad and rejoice, and give honour to him: for the marriage of the Lamb is come, and his wife hath made herself ready.

. . . Blessed are they which are called unto the marriage supper of the Lamb.
Revelation 19:7,9

Paul said, *. . . I have espoused you to one husband, that I may present you as a chaste virgin to Christ* (2 Cor. 11:2). The chaste virgin is the Church.

There will be a union between Christ and His Church. In Ephesians 5:31 when God says, *For this cause shall a man leave his father and mother, and shall be joined unto his wife . . .*, He is talking about the union. The verse continues, *. . . and they two shall be one flesh.*

Suddenly Christ and His Church will be one in the Rapture. When Christ comes and takes the Church, we will be joined with Him and go to this great wedding supper.

The union between Christ and His Church will not be organic or physical, but mystical. However, each time a man and woman—Christian or not—have relations, they are enacting at the human, physical level this beautiful and mystical union in a type and shadow of Christ and His Church.

Satan Perverts the Normal Union

Somebody has said that there is only one way to do right, and that's to do right. But there are infinitely varied ways of doing wrong.

Satan has an antagonism towards normalcy. One psychologist did some research on perversions, deviations, and abberations. He listed two thousand ways a person could have sexual release other than the normal way God intended between a man and a woman.

People will try any of the two thousand deviations from the norm. After they have experimented, they get satiated, jaded, discontented, bored, and frustrated. They say the same thing one famous movie star said just before he died, "I'm looking for a new thrill." They are bored with the old one.

One of the things that gives away Satan's program is the boredom and monotony that goes along with it. Boredom and monotony is now a modern-day problem. Books are written on escaping from boredom.

4
Danger:
Breakdown of Roles

The world is moving toward the era of the Antichrist. The Antichrist will be bisexual, inspiring both men and women to fall madly in love with him. Men will have a despicable love for him, and women, an abnormal love. Already, we are on the threshold of a complete breakdown in male and female roles.

Male and Female Roles Cross

Sociologists say that in 1880 the male/female poles began to cross in America. Approximately 1968 to 1970 the masculine male and the feminine female met somewhere in the middle.

What is known as "unisex" resulted: Men and women began to look alike.

I heard about a preacher who performed a marriage ceremony for two shaggy-looking creatures. When he had finished, he said, "Would the man please kiss the woman?" He couldn't tell who was who!

The Male Abdicates Leadership

Today in America the male has abdicated his leadership. When he surrendered his masculine role as priest, leader, and guide to his family, the female stepped out of her role and became the aggressor. The Women's Liberation Movement has caused the woman to become a fierce competitor. We have a matriarchal society; Mom is in the driver's seat.

You may have heard about the little girl who pointed to the man standing next to her mother and said, "Mama, who's that?'' The mother answered, ''Oh, that's Daddy. He brings home the check; we take it from there.''

Situation comedies on TV reflect the change in the role of the American male. The husband is usually depicted as a blundering idiot—the one who makes all the mistakes. The wife is always the one who saves the day. The list of situation comedies which show the man to be absolutely unnecessary to his family is lengthy.

Did you hear what happened when Saint Peter told the men in heaven to form two lines? Saint Peter said, ''I want every man who was the head of his house to get in one line and every man who wasn't to get in the other.'' The men did as he said.

Saint Peter walked happily down the heads-of-the-house line looking over the masculine, gutsy men. Then he came to a frail, little Casper-

Milquetoast-type man, obviously henpecked. Disgusted, Saint Peter asked, "What are you doing in this line?"

The man answered, "My wife told me to get in it."

Because the male has stepped out of his role, he is hounded with feelings of inadequacy and faces horrible fears of inferiority and insufficiency. In trying to find his identity or escape from pressures of an unhappy home situation, the American male spends billions of dollars a year on sports equipment. He buys golf clubs, fishing poles, hunting licenses, and boats, searching for identity.

Because the female has stepped out of character, she too is frustrated.

A breakdown in male and female roles is dangerous. It is one of the things that causes a civilization to decline.

Destruction of Civilizations

The Book of Daniel describes the reigns of Nebuchadnezzar and his grandson, Belshazzar. Nebuchadnezzar, the first leader of the Babylonian Empire, was all man—masculine and gutsy. Belshazzar was not. The Bible tells of a party, hosted by Belshazzar, that had tones of effeminency. During Belshazzar's time on the throne, the Babylonian Empire declined.

The Spartan army of ancient Greece was known for its fortitude. Eating only one meal a day, the Spartans conquered the world. When the Greek man became effeminate and the Greek woman, masculine, the Greek Empire declined.

Some groups say that Russia is America's enemy. But Russia is not: America is her own enemy. The emphasis in America is on voluptuous living, on permissiveness. She is one big drinking parlor from coast to coast. By her own moral depravity, America is weakening her moral fibre and destroying herself.

Historians point out that twenty-one civilizations have fallen since the year one. Of these, nineteen have destroyed themselves.

Something that causes a civilization to destroy itself is an emphasis on leisure time activities, amusement, and entertainment.

Today in America there is talk about going to a four-day work week. This will compound problems, not solve them. There will be more alcoholics and suicides than ever before. Leisure time will only lead to emptiness, boredom, loneliness, and life without a purpose.

Frivolous living takes the moral fibre out of a civilization. The male and female roles break down. The civilization begins to decline. The great Roman Empire began with a gladiator, but ended with a drinking bout.

An Island of Normalcy

A husband and wife need to assume their roles as outlined in the Bible. The Christian marriage is an island of faith in a sea of unbelief, an island of normalcy in a sea of perversion.

Before Jesus Christ comes back, there will be a polarization between the Christian and the non-Christian. The Christian will represent everything that is wholesome, normal, beautiful, and right. The non-Christian will be a stronghold of every imaginable unclean thing. Before it's over, the Christian marriage will be the only normal thing left on the face of the earth.

This is not a depressive thing. Look at it from a missionary standpoint. People whose worlds are caving in—

their marriages have collapsed; their kids, bored to tears and looking for a new thrill, are in trouble—will be drawn to a home based and maintained on Christian principles. The Christian home is going to serve as a great soul-winning institution.

A Christian couple had better re-evaluate their marriage. They should make sure that they are following the chain of command described in the Bible.

5

The Chain of Command

But I would have you know, that the head of every man is Christ; and the head of the woman is the man; and the head of Christ is God.

1 Corinthians 11:3

In this verse God gives us a chain of command for the home.

The Head of Jesus Is the Father-God

For the thirty-three and one-half years that Jesus was on earth, He fit harmoniously into His mother and father's home. But He also answered to His heavenly Father.

Jesus never resisted His Father-God or opposed Him, but always surrendered His will in every decision. He said, . . . *not my will, but thine, be done* (Luke 22:42).

Jesus showed us how to operate in the chain of command. He was in harmony with His Father, but was not a robot or computerized. He was a separate entity, a separate personality and individual.

The Head of Every Man Is Jesus

According to 1 Corinthians 11:3, every man—Christian or not—answers to Jesus. This is a beautiful thing.

Jesus speaks to men while they are flying airplanes, driving trucks and taxicabs, and working in factories. He speaks to them while they are sitting in bars. Many wives are crying out for their husbands to get saved, and Jesus is talking to these men.

Once at an interchurch gathering, I was scheduled to speak in a building that had a circular bar in the middle. As I was walking through the bar, I passed a man who was drinking beer and watching a football game on TV. Jesus said to me, "I've been talking to that fellow all day. I'll tell you what I've been saying to him; then I want you to go and tell him."

When halftime came on, I went up to the man. I said, "Hey, I want to tell you something. I'm with the group who loves the Lord that's meeting here. I don't know if you know this but Jesus loves you. I know that Jesus has been talking to you all morning."

The guy started crying. He said, "Yeah, you know, He has."

I said, "I want to tell you what He's been telling you." And I did. We had a prayer meeting right in that bar! Even with his hands around a glass of beer, that man was answering to Jesus.

The Head of the Wife Is the Husband

The wife answers to the husband. People involved in the Women's

Liberation Movement have opposed this idea because they have misunderstood the reason for it. They have seen as its purpose to reduce the woman to an inferior role. This is not true. The wife answers to her husband for her own protection. Submission is not slavery; it is security.

The Woman's Covering

First Corinthians 11:10 says, *For this cause ought the woman to have power* ("covering" AMP[5]) *on her head because of the angels.* The original Greek for the word *power* in this verse is *exousia*. It means "authority."

In verse 15 Paul talks about the covering of hair being the crowning glory of the woman's head. Because of this, some of the legalistic churches believe that the covering referred to in verse 10 is the woman's hair. Some women who were unable to grow big, bushy heads of hair have been badgered as a result.

The covering that protects the woman isn't necessarily the head of hair or a veil as some believe. The covering, the *exousia*, is the husband.

Every woman needs an "authority." Our society used to protect the woman much more than it does now. At one time a single woman was protected by her father, brother, or church. The married woman was protected by her husband. Nobody could indiscriminately walk up to any woman and just start talking.

At one time I tried to play cupid and get single people together. Married people sometimes think, *We've got to get the singles paired off.* But some people don't need to get married, and shouldn't, until later. Proverbs 24:27 says to prepare ourselves for the future, to get our careers established. *Prepare thy work without, and make it fit for thyself in the field; and afterwards build thine house* (your family). Then we are ready for matrimony. Some people would jeopardize their careers by rushing prematurely into marriage. Take my advice: It's better not to play cupid.

Today's church does offer spiritual, mental, and physical protection to its widows, divorcees, unmarried career girls, and spinsters. The person submitted to a church, its teachings, policies, and doctrines is guaranteed all kinds of protection in God's Word. The harmonious relationship to a Bible-believing church can be a spiritual covering to a single woman, just as a husband is to a wife. (See. Ps. 84:1-4.)

Often a woman has not realized what a protection her husband is to her in many different areas of life. He covers her from the elements, evil people and unhappy neighbors, the children, and the angels. And he is to care lovingly for her.

Paul said, *Husbands, love your wives, even as Christ also loved the church* (Eph.

5:25). The Greek word for *love* in this verse is *agape*. In other words, "Husbands, be unselfish and sacrificial. Give of yourselves to your wives just as Christ gave Himself to the Church." A woman should appreciate answering to the man; it is for her own protection.

Protection from the Elements

Every time a man says to a woman, "Will you marry me?" he is telling her: "I'm going to put a roof over your head. You won't have to brave the elements; I'll take you out of them."

With every proposal goes an automatic guarantee for a house to protect the woman from the elements.

Protection from Evil People

In some areas of the country, a particularly sad thing happens at night: Degenerate people drive the highways just to look for trouble.

One time a girl ran out of gas on a freeway at two o'clock in the morning. A highway patrolman driving the other way saw her go to the emergency telephone and pick up the receiver. Then he saw her get into a car that had stopped. She was never seen again.

That girl had a habit of forgetting to check her gas gauge. Her boyfriend said later that all day long he had a feeling he ought to put some gas in her car. Her brother had also had the same feeling. But neither one checked with her. When she ran out of gasoline, an evil person picked her up.

Somebody should have covered the girl. A husband knows where his wife is at all times so that he can cover her. If she is ever exposed to evil people, he is available to get to her or to send help.

Protection from Unhappy Neighbors

One time when I was visiting some people, an unhappy neighbor came storming up to their house. Seeing him coming, the man hid in the bedroom and sent his wife to the door. I thought, *I've never seen such a chicken in my life!* The man certainly wasn't assuming his proper role.

In another situation a lady answered her door to find a disgruntled neighbor there. When he began talking, the lady just smiled. (Some ladies would have gone for the guy's jugular vein.)

"Would you talk to my husband?" she said. That was the smartest thing she could have done. She knew that her husband was her protection.

Protection from the Children

As we will see later, the children answer to the mother. But the husband should cover his wife from the children.

Sometimes you hear children make disrespectful comments to their mother like this: "Mom, you're an old fuddy-duddy out of the Paleolithic Age—an antique. You're not with it." They also criticize her cooking and make demands: "I don't like what you cooked for dinner," or "I want the car. Why can't I have it?"

No man should let his kids treat their mother like this.

Pastor Larry Christenson tells about a time when he was disrespectful to his mother. Correcting him about something, she said, "I don't like your behavior, Larry. You've got to change."

He answered, "You're a dummy!" Then he turned and walked off, unaware that his dad had just walked in the door and heard him.

A highly successful football coach, Larry's father is gutsy—all man. He stormed in, grabbed the front of Larry's shirt, and lifted him off the floor. Looking Larry straight in the eyes, he asked, "Who's a dummy?"

Larry answered quickly, *"I'm* a dummy! *I'm* a dummy!"

This is a good example of a husband covering his wife from their children.

Every man should periodically arrange adequate care for the children, then take his wife away from the telephone, the neighbors, the relatives, and the chores of the home. He should take her away just so they can get more closely acquainted. Some of our most fun, intimate, happy, and fulfilling times have been when my wife and I have gone off somewhere for recreation and relaxation. A man should take his wife away from the home scene as a part of protecting her from the children.

Protection from the Angels

As we saw before in 1 Corinthians 11:10, Paul said, *For this cause ought the woman to have power on her head because of the angels.*

One day I began to wonder if Paul was referring here to good angels or bad angels. For my own information I examine references written from different viewpoints and have many commentaries on the book of First Corinthians. Half these commentaries state that Paul was talking about the good angels. Knowing nothing but law and order, the good angels never question a command.

For each angel that fell with Satan, two others stayed. These two angels help you. When you drive down the freeway, one angel is on your left fender and one on your right to protect you.

If the speed limit is fifty-five miles per hour and you are driving under that limit, the angels are with you. If you break the speed limit by going sixty-five miles per hour, the angels jump off. (Have you ever noticed that when you speed up your car, the front end gets lighter? That's because the angels have jumped off!)

If good angels know only harmony, they will be jarred at anything in the Church that creates disharmony. The Lord hates things that bring disharmony. This is why He hates *a proud look, a lying* (gossiping) *tongue, and hands that shed innocent blood . . . feet that be swift in running to mischief . . . and he that soweth discord among brethren* (Prov. 6:17-19).

It is a deadly thing when a person sows discord among the brethren. One little voice can severely disturb the harmony of God and start discord in the Church.

In the Women's Liberation Movement, there is a thing known as "male antagonism." Sigmund Freud defined this as an envy a woman has in which she never forgives God for not creating her as a man.

55

these: ''*Me* submit to a man? Never! I can do what any man can do better, because I'm better than any man.'' These women refused to accept the chain of command.

As one pastor told me: ''All the problems I have seen in twenty-five years of ministry can be traced to one type of personality: the woman with male antagonism. She's dominating, domineering, and overbearing. This type of woman will not submit to her husband. She holds her children in fear and terror. She has never accepted the leadership of the pastor, contesting him on every point. She's never really surrendered to Jesus.''

Paul said that one modern-day problem would be silly women. (2 Tim. 3:6.) The woman who won't accept the leadership of a husband as a priest in the Church is going to lay herself wide open to every kind of demonic manifestation.

Children Answer to the Wife

According to Proverbs, chapter 31, the children answer to the wife. The man is not free from the responsibilities of raising and disciplining the children, but the mother is the major influence in their lives. She is the one who gives them the strong religious and moral training. She is their main teacher about the principles and incidents of life.

The chain of command is this:

Jesus answers to God the Father.

The man answers to Jesus.

The wife answers to the man.

The children answer to the wife.

We can see that God's thinking in creating the chain of command was not to place the woman in a second-class role or to reduce her to nothing. God set up the chain of command for the woman's own protection.

A woman who heard Pastor Dennis Bennett's wife teach at a women's gathering spoke with her afterwards and said, ''You advertise yourself as 'Mrs. Dennis Bennett.' That's wrong. Using 'Mrs.' makes you second class.''

A woman with this type of attitude can be jarring or offending the angels of the Lord at the same time she is in church worshiping God. The angels know only God's law and order. The resentful, antagonistic, envious woman is in rebellion to the chain of command —she is out of harmony and is offending those good angels.

What happens when the woman refuses the chain of command by not submitting to the leadership of the man? Evil angels get through, and the woman gets seduced by these evil spirits.

Many false cults were started by women. Often these women had a male antagonism. They made statements like

6
The Male's Drive To Succeed

Every man is motivated by a driving force, a strong desire to succeed. This is part of the ego. The word *ego* is a Greek word for "I" or self.

Let me add another definition. An egotist is a person who is always talking about himself when you wish he would talk about you. He thinks that had he not been born, people would have wondered why.

Somebody once said that the codfish lays 20,000 eggs at once and doesn't say a word; the hen lays one egg and cackles all day. Egotists are always cackling about their accomplishments.

Demoralizing Failure

God put into the man this driving desire to succeed. It is the greatest motivator in the world. The only thing more demoralizing to a man than being hounded with feelings of failure is actual failure. And modern-day life sets up the man either to think of himself as a failure or to fail.

Because of the population explosion, the man is no longer an individual—he is just an IBM card. Ruthless competition in the business world is taking its toll on the man. Underhanded business practices birthed by power struggles increase the chances for failure. The mandatory retirement age forces the man to step down, giving him a feeling of failure.

Most retired people are irritable and mad at the whole world because retirement was forced on them. I lived in a town of retired people. The town is called the foothills of heaven because it is the last jumping off place, the last stop, before heaven. People go there to die.

Retirement is demoralizing. A man in the prime of his life is handed a watch, given a little farewell dinner, and shoved out.

In the competitive commercial world inflation adds to a man's sense of failure. Technological advancement replaces him with computers. Every eager beaver on the job is trying to get his promotion.

A business executive making around $40,000 per year came to me for counseling.

"I want out," he said.

"What for?" I said.

"In my office, there's always a cross-fire, a power struggle, among the executives. Everybody is trying to climb over everybody else to get a promotion.

61

It's a hassle. I never look forward to going to work. I'd just a soon buy a car wash and stand there spraying cars for 50¢ a car."

Love Is a Conquest

The man goes to work in what is known as the rodent derby or rat race. After facing that howling mob, he comes home bleeding. He needs Band-Aids, lots of affection and love.

He steps inside the door. The first thing his wife says is, "Don't say anything. I want to tell you about the kind of day I had." No wonder the guy spends a lot of time at the bowling alley.

A common remark that women make during counseling sessions is, "My husband wants relations far more frequently than I do. What can I do?"

The woman who says something like this does not understand the man's driving desire to succeed. The woman must understand that to the man love is not a sentimental thing but a conquest, a part of the desire of his ego to succeed.

God Meant Man to Pursue

It is true that the man's frequency ratio (desire for relations) is greater than the woman's. God deliberately created man to be this way so that, of the two, he would be the aggressor. God meant for a man to pursue his wife.

A baby cannot be conceived without a tremendous amount of aggressive drive on the part of the male sperm. Without that drive, the sperm cannot reach the egg to fertilize it. Some couples never have children because the sperm doesn't have enough driving force and aggression within it.

The man has aggressiveness within him: he is a driver, a pusher, a pursuer. When I was a single evangelist, someone gave me this sage advice: ''As a male, you will never be satisfied being pursued. To be satisfied and happy, *you* must pursue.''

When the man is making love to his wife, he is at the height of his glory. His ego is at its best. At that particular moment, he feels needed, necessary. His wife's love and affection make him feel self-respect and success.

7

The Wife's Ministry

Many a wife has been baffled when her husband struts around the house flexing his muscles and pulling in his stomach. She watches as he looks admiringly at himself in the mirror as though he were God's gift to women.

Many women who have never understood the male ego feel it is their job in life to squash it. These women don't understand that when their husbands fail, they fail. When their husbands succeed, they succeed.

Some wives think they are in a big contest to outwit their husbands. They are always trying to figure out how to keep him at arm's length. They come up with all kinds of sneaky excuses to avoid sex: ''Not tonight, honey—I've got a headache,'' or ''Mama is coming over soon,'' or ''The kids aren't feeling well.''

When the man goes home feeling like a failure and his wife reminds him of what a failure she thinks he is, he has nothing working for him. Then, all of a sudden, there is friction in the marriage.

Building Self-Respect

Man was made out of the dust of the earth, so he is kind of earthy and like clay—''a clod of the sod.'' Woman is a little more refined. She was made twice—first out of the dust of the earth, then from man's rib.

I heard about the night Adam stayed out late. At first Eve was worried, but by two o'clock in the morning, she was steamed! She paced the floor until she heard him coming in. But instead of yelling, ''Where have you been? Is there another woman?'' she didn't say one critical word.

As a good, intelligent wife, Eve didn't tell Adam she had been anxious. She just waited until he fell asleep, then she counted his ribs!

A woman doesn't need to "count her husband's ribs" or keep him humble. She needs to realize that when her husband proposed to her he was saying, "No other woman in the world has anything I want or can offer me anything that you can't offer. I'm happy with you. I want to live with you. I'm not interested in anybody but you. I want to love you; I want you to love me. I want to respect you; I want you to respect me." He still feels that way.

The intelligent woman who understands a man's basic need for love, and especially for self-respect, looks at her husband for what he is: A little kid who has grown up. She has discovered that he breaks easily, that he needs a lot of affection, patting, and reassurance. Her attitude is, "I'm going to saturate him with kindness and love."

Mrs. Dale Carnegie told about a man who walked into his home and handed his wife twenty dollars.

"What's this for?" his wife asked.

The man answered, "Honey, I've got sad news. We're wiped out."

This man owned a ten-million-dollar empire; but because of wrong investments and a fluctuating stock market, the whole thing had collapsed.

"We don't own this house or that car out there in the driveway anymore," the man continued. "The cabin, the boat, the country club membership, the stocks and bonds, the jewelry—everything is gone. We don't have anything.

"I want you to take this twenty dollars, go home to your mother, and wait for me. I'm going to go out and try

to recover financially. When I make it,
I'll send for you."

Some women would have said,
"How could you do this to me? What
am I going to tell all the ladies at the
country club? I'll never be able to face
them again!"

But this woman said, "If you go out
that door, I'll go with you. If you sleep
under a bridge tonight or go to a dollar-
a-night flophouse, I'll be there with
you. I don't want to go home to my
mother. My life isn't the house, the car,
the boat, the country club, the mink
stole, and the jewelry. I'm not married
to those things; I'm married to *you*. My
life is *you*; I believe in *you*. You'll recover
and when you do, I want to be there."

Mrs. Carnegie said, "That kind of
confidence had that man back in the
race in a year." That intelligent woman
realized she was a minister. Her
ministry was one of building self-
respect in her husband.

The Wife Is the Equalizer

In this age of tension, many men are so bowed down with anxieties and pressures that they are not able to perform as they should, even becoming sexually apathetic.

A loving wife can be the great equalizer. Many a man is demoralized in every area of life—he is unhappy about business pressures, his financial and social status, transportation, his own physical condition, and his intelligence. If that man has a wife who understands his basic needs for affection and love, the aggression and conquest he uses in love-making can compensate for every blow of life.

There is another reason why the wife's ministry to her husband is so important.

The Bible says that in the last days men's hearts will fail them for fear. (Luke 21:26.) In the late sixties and early seventies, four out of five American men between the ages of 35 and 55 suffered heart attacks. They were caught in the rodent derby. But the Christian is not.

No Christian need have a heart attack.

Proverbs 16:7 says, *When a man's ways please the Lord, he maketh even his enemies to be at peace with him.*

Proverbs 22:29 says, *Seest thou a man diligent in his business? he shall stand before kings; he shall not stand before mean men.* He will never waste his time on nonentities.

Psalm 75:6,7 says, *For promotion cometh neither from the east, nor from the west, nor from the south. But God is the judge: he putteth down one, and setteth up another.* Promotion comes from the Lord.

The only way for a man to survive the vicious, ruthless, competitive world is to stand on the security that God gave him. As long as God wants him on a job, no devil in hell can fire him from it.

If that job phases out, the Christian knows the Lord has something better. His attitude is: "I'm not worried. The Lord will provide for my family and me each day. We have put our whole trust in God and His Word. His promises have never failed us and never will. Circumstances do not dictate to us. We're more than conquerors."

The wife can help her husband keep this attitude through her ministry of building his self-respect. It is during times of intimacy that a wife is actually providing her husband with the things he needs the most—self-respect and self-confidence. The wife's ability to supply these ingredients should not be taken lightly. She alone can offset all the negatives that are stacked against him, trying to finish him off.

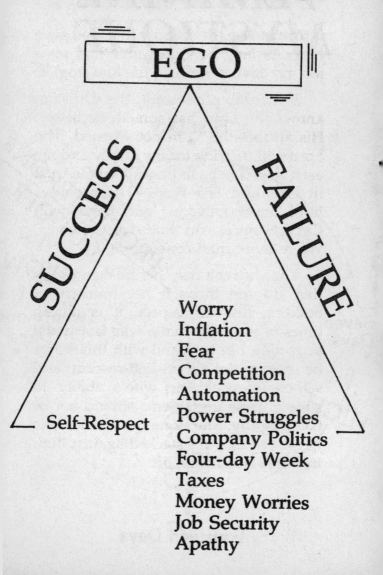

FEMININE MYSTIQUE

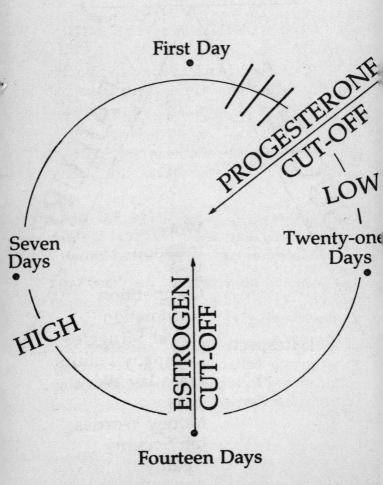

8
The Feminine Mystique

One day when Dad comes home, his wife meets him at the door, puts her arms around him, and says, "Hello, lover!"

He scratches his head and says, "I wonder what I've done to deserve that?"

Two weeks later when he comes home, his wife says, "Don't touch me, you brute! I'm going home to Mother."

Again he scratches his head and says, "I wonder what I've done to deserve that?"

He hasn't done anything. A woman's behavior can be completely attributed to a chemical reaction going on inside her.

Highs and Lows

According to doctors, ninety percent of American women have an ovulation cycle of approximately twenty-five to twenty-eight days in duration.

A chemical balance occurs during the first fourteen days of the cycle which causes the woman to have a sense of well-being. During these fourteen days two hormones, estrogen and progesterone, circulate through her body. (You must realize that all this information deals with approximates, due to much variance within women in general.) This is a high for her. She is tender and sensitive, affectionate and cuddly, responsive to candlelight and guitar music.

The egg forms in the ovary and moves into the fallopian tube. When the egg reaches a place in the uterus where it can be fertilized, her body stops producing estrogen. This occurs in the middle of the cycle. During the next fourteen days, she experiences a chemical imbalance, a low.

Her body still produces progesterone until the twenty-fifth or twenty-sixth day. Just before the cycle is completed, the progesterone cuts off suddenly. For the next two to five days she can be jittery, nervous, and moody. She can get upset easily and cry.

During those two to five days, the average man usually does something like this: About three o'clock in the afternoon he calls his wife and says, "I'm bringing the boss and twenty other men home for dinner, so fix a big spaghetti supper." This almost gives his wife one response: the urge to kill!

Dwell According to Knowledge

First Peter 3:7 says, . . . *Husbands, dwell with them* (your wives) *according to knowledge, giving honour unto the wife, as unto the weaker vessel, and as being heirs together of the grace of life; that your prayers be not hindered*. A husband should know that his wife will be experiencing some jittery days until the cycle starts again.

One man I know makes no demands on his wife during this time. He tells her, "Honey, I want you to feel good and know that I appreciate you. I know things aren't at their best, but I love you. Let's go out for dinner."

He takes her out for dinner and later buys her a pair of shoes. His wife has a closet full of shoes, but she thinks he is the world's greatest hero!

The man who wins understands that his wife's emotional makeup is geared to this twenty-eight day ovulation cycle. She will have a balance (an affectionate high) and an imbalance (a depressive low). The man who is a hero in the eyes of his wife is the considerate, thoughtful man. He understands that during her unaffectionate times she doesn't think any less of him. It's just that her actions reflect the imbalance. He knows that time is on his side.

The man who loses makes all kinds of demands on his jittery wife during the imbalance.

Redeemed from the Curse of the Law

Many Spirit-filled women do not have the extreme elation and depression other women have. Jesus has changed this for them.

These women know that Christ has redeemed them from the curse of the Law. (Gal. 3:13.) Even though the chemistry is at work in their bodies, they have some other things working for them—the love of God and the power of the Holy Ghost.

9
Prefer One Another

Many thoughtless and inconsiderate husbands and wives make unrealistic demands on each other. Selfishness is a major cause of friction in marriage.

Consideration

The wife hath not power of her own body, but the husband: and likewise also the husband hath no power of his own body, but the wife.

1 Corinthians 7:4

The Apostle Paul is saying that the husband does not exist for his own gratification, but for his wife's happiness: he is here to fulfill her. The wife is not here for her own fulfillment, but for her husband's. To be happily married, a man and a woman need to look out for each other's best interests.

The key to happiness in marriage is consideration. Husbands and wives need to be unselfish, preferring one another.

When I was twenty-five years old, I married for the first time. I was aggressive, impetuous, impatient, impulsive, and fiercely competitive. I steamrolled through every situation, pushing people around. As a husband I was thoughtless and inconsiderate.

My wife contracted cancer of the colon. Just a few weeks later, she was gone. There I was, 34 years old with a 5-year-old son. We were in a state of shock. (Nobody ever puts bereavement on their schedule.)

About that time I read some material which stated that an evangelist should not get married. It said that an evangelist has no permanence, stability, or security to offer a woman and that his being away from home so much would not be fair to his wife and children.

I was speaking 400 to 500 times a year and traveling a great deal. I had nothing to offer a woman in the way of security. I thought, *Maybe the Lord wants me to go through the rest of my life as a eunuch.*

About six months after my wife passed away, my boy came to me crying. He said, "Dad, I heard your sermon called 'Ask, Seek, and Knock.' Do you believe it?"

I said, "Yes."

"If we ask for anything, will the Lord give it to us?"

"Yes."

"Well, I want to ask for something."

"What do you want to ask for?"

"I want to ask for a mommie."

Then I started crying and said, "Well, I want to ask for one, too!"

We were two little kids crying our hearts out, so we started praying for a mommie.

I began reading the Song of Solomon. The Lord gave me a most beautiful understanding of it, of Christ and His Bride. (Everybody should read that beautiful love story in one of the modern translations.) I was overawed with it.

"Lord," I said, "that's the most beautiful love story I've ever read. I wish I could have a life like that."

The Lord spoke to me and said, "You're going to. You're going to have a beautiful life."

I went to Artesia, California, to hold a revival. After sharing my understanding of the Song of Solomon with the pastor there, I said, "I believe the Lord is going to let this beautiful love story happen in my life." I didn't know it was going to happen right there in Artesia!

That evening, I went to the sponsoring pastor's house. When I walked in, there she was—my future wife Betty. She was a registered nurse and dressed in her uniform. When I saw her, my eyes dilated, my blood pressure went up, my knees began to knock, and I took "a turn for the *nurse!*"

Before she knew what hit her, I had put a ring on her finger, rushed her down the aisle, and married her!

I was introducing Betty to a whole new type of existence. She had never been married before. Her total church experience consisted of five years at a church in St. Louis and another five years at one in Artesia. We began our marriage by towing a thirty-foot mobile home all over the United States doing forty-four straight weeks of evangelistic work!

In those days there were no good mobile home parks; they were all gypsy camps. We got into some camps where prostitution and gambling were going on; also we had peeping toms.

Every week we would be facing a new set of people, a new environment, and a new type of housing arrangement. This would be the way our life together would always be.

I had been married the first time for nine years, then was without any marital activity during that following year of bereavement. But instead of being concerned about my own happiness when I married Betty, I had a compulsive desire to make her happy. The Lord put within me a desire to be thoughtful and considerate to her. I wanted to give her security, privacy, and contentment.

In those early days, as we travelled in that mobile home, I learned the greatest lesson in life: kindness begets kindness, thoughtfulness begets thoughtfulness, consideration begets consideration, and love begets love.

I found that in looking out for Betty's best interests, I got fringe benefits—the preferential treatment. While I was looking out for *her* happiness, she was looking out for *mine*. Oh, what a discovery! Betty is always motivated with the same thought, *What can I do to make my husband happy?*

I would wake up to find that she had brought me breakfast in bed, including squeezed orange juice. I never had it so good!

One Sunday morning I woke up to see her shining my shoes. I'm an old G.I., and every G.I. shines his own shoes.

"What are you doing?" I asked.

"We're running late," she answered. "I want to get you going."

"You don't have to shine my shoes!"

"I love it! I love you."

Being sentimental, I came unglued.

I don't believe that a woman should shine her husband's shoes or that a man should wash his wife's underwear. There are certain things men and women should do for themselves. The point is that we both were doing everything we could to make the other happy.

Keep Courting

Some husbands and wives become miserable together because they let up on their courtship after they marry. Once someone gives his heart to Jesus, he doesn't just sit around waiting for the Rapture. Getting saved isn't the end of life in the Christian walk: it's the beginning. A husband and wife need to continue working on their marriage just as they do their Christian walk.

Did you read about the fellow who hadn't kissed his wife in fifteen years?

He shot three other guys for trying, but never kissed her himself!

I heard about a businessman who recorded this on tape: "I love you, I love you, I love you." On his wedding day he handed the tape to his new wife and said, "Honey, I'm awfully busy. If you want to know how I feel, play this."

One man came home and asked his wife, "Who's that big guy standing in the corner?"

"That's Junior," she said. "He grew up while you were out making money."

Many unmarried women starve themselves to stay a trim and petite size 12. Once they get married, immediately they gain twenty pounds. Six months later they say to their husbands, "None of my clothes fit." Then the husbands have to pay for all the new clothes.

The man gets married and lets down; the woman gets married and lets down. Each year thousands of men leave their homes to get a drink at the corner bar but never come back. A large percentage of ladies do the same thing.

In the non-Christian world marriage is breaking down and disappearing. Society wants to replace it with a new type of living, a new syndrome. Every Christian husband and wife need to ignore this new attitude and work on their personal lives, looking out for each other's happiness.

Marriage doesn't have to be a series of shouting matches or a battleground full of friction and turmoil. Marriage can and should be happy. A happy marriage is heaven on earth; an unhappy marriage is hell on earth. Romance has to be kept alive through a continual process of courtship.

Remember: kindness begets kindness, thoughtfulness begets thoughtfulness, consideration begets consideration, and love begets love.

Notes

1. *The Septuagint Bible*, trans. by Charles Thomson (Indian Hills, CO: Falcon's Wing Press, 1960), p. 4.

2. Helen Spurrell, *A Translation of the Old Testament Scriptures* (London: James Nisbet and Co., 1885), p. 2.

3. James Strong, S.T.D., LL.D., *The Exhaustive Concordance of the Bible* (Nashville: Abingdon, 1980), Heb. and Chaldee Dict., p. 27.

4. *The Living Bible* (Wheaton: Tyndale House, 1971), p. 2.

5. *The Amplified Bible, New Testament* (La Habra, CA: The Lockman Foundation, 1954, 1958), p. 261.